Living in God's Love ❧ Guided

Love ❧ Shaped by God's Love

God's Love ❧ Confident in G

Living in God's Love ❧ Guided

Love ❧ Shaped by God's Love

God's Love ❧ Confident in G

Living in God's Love ❧ Guided

Love ❧ Shaped by God's Love

God's Love ❧ Confident in G

Living in God's Love ❧ Guided

Love ❧ Shaped by God's Love

God's Love ❧ Confident in G

Living in God's Love ❧ Guided

Love ❧ Shaped by God's Love

God's Love ❧ Confident in

Growing in God's Love ❧ Strengthened by G
Complete in God's Love ❧ Create
Growing in God's Love ❧ Strengthened by G
Complete in God's Love ❧ Create
Growing in God's Love ❧ Strengthened by G
Complete in God's Love ❧ Create
Growing in God's Love ❧ Strengthened by G
Complete in God's Love ❧ Create
Growing in God's Love ❧ Strengthened by G
Complete in God's Love ❧ Create

God's Love
for You

HOPE AND ENCOURAGEMENT FOR LIFE

BILLY GRAHAM

Copyright © 2007 by Billy Graham

Published by J. Countryman, a division of Thomas Nelson, Inc, Nashville, Tennessee 37214.

Compiled and edited by Terri Gibbs

The contents of this book are taken from *The Journey: How to Live by Faith in an Uncertain World* by Billy Graham (W Publishing Group, 2006), with additional notations by the author.

Unless otherwise indicated, all Scripture quotations in this book are from the New King James Version (NKJV) ©1979, 1980, 1982, 1992, Thomas Nelson, Inc., Publisher and are used by permission.

Other Scripture references are from the New International Version of the Bible (NIV) © 1984 by the International Bible Society. Used by permission of Zondervan Bible Publishers. The King James Version of the Bible (KJV).

Designed by The Design Works Group, Inc., Sisters, Oregon.

ISBN 13: 978-1-4041-0406-8

Printed and bound in Belgium

Contents

Foreword

The more I read the Bible, the more I realize that love is God's supreme attribute. Behind every dealing God has with us is His perfect love. It was love that made Him create us, and it was love that caused Him to send His Son to redeem us. His love pursues us and draws us to Himself, and His love will some day take His children into His presence forever.

As with other aspects of His nature, we have a difficult time fully understanding God's love. For one thing, the word "Love" has come to mean almost anything today. We say we "love" ice cream or the color of a car, or we say we "love" an entertainer or celebrity (although we've never met them, and never will). But God's love is far deeper than this. His love is not a passing fancy or superficial emotion; it is a profound and unshakable commitment that seeks what is best for us. Human love may change or fade; God's love never will. He says to us, "I have loved you with an everlasting love; I have drawn you with loving-kindness" (Jer. 31:3 NIV).

Don't sentimentalize God's love, however. God's love isn't a warm, fuzzy feeling that ignores sin or shuns judgment. God's holiness demands that sin be punished—

but God's love has provided the way of redemption through Christ. If it weren't for God's love we would have no hope, either in this life or the life to come.

But there *is* hope, because He loves us! In the following pages I invite you to join me in discovering God's profound and abundant love for you.

Billy Graham

Complete in
God's Love

In this is love, not that we loved God,
but that He loved us.

1 JOHN 4:10

"I am the God of your father Abraham;
do not fear, for I am with you."

GENESIS 26:24

The LORD,
He is the One who goes before you.
He will be with you,
He will not leave you nor forsake you;
do not fear nor be dismayed.

DEUTERONOMY 31:8

"Lo, I am with you always, even to
the end of the age."

MATTHEW 28:20

When you pass through the waters,
I will be with you; and through the rivers,
they shall not overflow you.

ISAIAH 43:2

God Journeys with Us

God could have created us—and then abandoned us and forgotten all about us. Many people, in fact, believe this is exactly what God must have done, or at least they act as if He did. They assume God isn't interested in them—so why should they be interested in Him? To them God is distant, remote, unconcerned about the problems and decisions they face every day.

But this isn't true! God not only put us on this journey called life but He wants to join us on it, if we will only let Him. We don't need to be alone, for He is with us! The Psalmist asked, "Where can I go from your Spirit? Where can I flee from your presence? If I go up to the heavens, you are there; if I make my bed in the depths, you are there" (Psalm 139:7–8 NIV).

If we understand this truth, it gives us hope—hope that our lives *can* be different, because God cares about us and wants to help us. No matter what happens, God will never abandon us if our trust is in Him.

There is a friend
who sticks closer than a brother.

PROVERBS 18:24

"No longer do I call you servants . . .
but I have called you friends."

JOHN 15:15

"Greater love has no one than this,
than to lay down one's life for his friends."

JOHN 15:13

"You are My friends
if you do whatever I command you."

JOHN 15:14

Friends with God

Think of it: The infinite, all-powerful, holy God of the universe wants to be your friend! This is a staggering truth. He wants you to know him personally, and to discover what it means to walk with Him every day. He wants you to know He is with you, and He wants to have communication with you through His Word and through prayer. He wants to comfort you when you are upset or anxious, and to encourage you when you are dejected or depressed. He wants to guide you when you face difficult decisions, and He even wants to correct you when you are about to do something foolish or wrong.

Human friends may fail us, but God never will. He wants to be our friend, and for us to be His friends as well. Once you understand this, your life will never be the same.

No one is holy like the LORD,
for there is none besides You,
nor is there any rock like our God.

1 SAMUEL 2:2

Exalt the LORD our God,
and worship at His footstool—He is holy.

PSALM 99:5

Your Redeemer is the Holy One of Israel;
He is called the God of the whole earth.

ISAIAH 54:5

The Holiness of God

We are weak and imperfect, and we can scarcely grasp the overwhelming perfection and holiness of God. We have become so used to sin that we can't imagine anyone being absolutely perfect. But God is! The Bible says, "God is light; in him there is no darkness at all" (1 John 1:5, NIV). Because God is holy, He never does wrong—never. Occasionally we hear of someone who is exceptionally good and self-sacrificing—but even then, we know they aren't perfect. (If we think we are perfect, it just proves we aren't!) Only God is perfect and holy.

From one end of the Bible to the other, God reveals Himself as absolutely pure, without flaw or blemish of any kind. When Isaiah glimpsed a vision of God, he was overwhelmed by God's holiness—and his own sinfulness. He saw angels surrounding God's throne "calling to one another: 'Holy, holy, holy is the Lord Almighty; the whole earth is full of his glory'" (Isaiah 6:3 NIV).

Only when we understand the holiness of God will we understand the depth of our sin.

The peace of God,
which surpasses all understanding,
will guard your hearts and minds
through Christ Jesus.

PHILIPPIANS 4:7

You are complete in Him,
who is the head of all principality and power.

COLOSSIANS 2:10

Show me Your ways, O LORD;
teach me Your paths.

PSALM 25:4

Only God Can Satisfy

Why are we so restless? Why are we constantly searching for lasting peace and contentment, and yet never fully satisfied? "My friends all say I have everything anyone could ever want," one man wrote me recently, "but down inside I'm empty and restless. What's wrong with me?" Countless people could echo his cry, if they were honest.

The Bible says this happens to us for a very good reason: We are incomplete without God. If we leave Him out of our lives, we have an empty place in our souls, a yearning deep inside us that only God can satisfy. No matter how hard we try, if we ignore God that hollow place stays with us, and our search for lasting peace and happiness will be futile.

Centuries ago St. Augustine wrote, "You have made us for Yourself, O God, and our hearts are restless until they find their rest in You." Only God can satisfy the deepest longings of your heart.

*"You shall love the LORD your God
with all your heart, with all your soul,
and with all your mind."*

MATTHEW 22:37

*The Word became flesh and
dwelt among us.*

JOHN 1:14

*He who comes to God
must believe that He is, and that
He is a rewarder
of those who diligently seek Him.*

HEBREWS 11:6

Knowing God

Most speculations about God miss one very important truth: God *wants* us to know what He is like. We don't need to guess, because God has revealed Himself to us.

Suppose you decided you didn't want anyone to know you existed. What would you have to do? Not only would you have to avoid any contact with other people, but you'd have to be sure you didn't leave any evidence around that you existed. You couldn't even put out your trash or turn on a light! Just the smallest trace would indicate you existed—and the more clues you left behind, the more convinced people would be that you were real.

This is somewhat the way it is with God. We know He exists because He has left clues behind for us to discover. But there is a crucial difference: God isn't trying to hide from us. Quite the opposite: God wants us to know He exists. Not only that, He wants us to know what He is like. In other words, He wants to communicate with us!

He did not leave Himself without witness,
in that He did good, gave us rain from heaven
and fruitful seasons, filling our hearts
with food and gladness.

ACTS 14:17

Since the creation of the world
His invisible attributes are clearly seen,
being understood by the things that are made,
even His eternal power and Godhead.

ROMANS 1:20

I will meditate
on the glorious splendor of Your majesty,
and on Your wondrous works.

PSALM 145:5

God's Footprints

No matter where we look, we see God's footprints.

Look up on a starry night—and you will see the majesty and power of an infinite Creator. Recently I saw a report about some recent discoveries in astronomy. It reported that astronomers now believe there may be as many as 140 billion galaxies in the known universe, some over eleven billion light years away—and each containing at least several hundred billion stars. We can't begin to imagine such distances or quantities.

God's "footprints" are everywhere, if we will but see them.

Created by
God's Love

*God is love, and he who
abides in love abides in God,
and God in him.*

1 JOHN 4:16

*I will praise You,
for I am fearfully and wonderfully made;
marvelous are Your works,
and that my soul knows very well.*

PSALM 139:14

*So God created man in His own image; in the
image of God He created him;
male and female He created them.*

GENESIS 1:27

*Have we not all one Father?
Has not one God created us?*

MALACHI 2:10

Because of His Love

God made us because of His love.

On a human level we know that love needs an outlet—that is, it yearns to be expressed and shared. In a far greater way, God's love had to have an outlet—it had to be expressed, and it had to be shared. That is why God created Adam and Eve. And He created them in His image so they would have the ability to love also—to love each other, and to love Him. God is love—and now this wondrous characteristic of His personality was being given to Adam and Eve. What a gift! God created Adam and Eve out of love, and gave them the ability to love Him (and each other) in return.

God didn't make Adam and Eve because He was lonely, or because He needed someone to love Him in return. This is true with human love, but it isn't true with God. God is complete in Himself, and He lacks nothing. Just as an artist has a compelling urge to create a beautiful painting, or a skilled woodworker has a compelling urge to create a fine piece of furniture, so our loving God had a compelling urge to create humanity. His love was expressed in the creation of the human race.

Your hands have made me and fashioned me;
give me understanding, that
I may learn Your commandments.

PSALM 119:73

Your eyes saw my substance,
being yet unformed.
And in Your book they all were written,
the days fashioned for me,
when as yet there were none of them.

PSALM 139:16

We are His workmanship,
created in Christ Jesus for good works,
which God prepared beforehand
that we should walk in them.

EPHESIANS 2:10

God Chose to Give You Life

You aren't here by chance or by accident; you are here because God put you here. Long before the world was created God knew all about you, and He planned to give you life. From all eternity you were part of His plan. No, you didn't have any choice about whether or not you would be born—but God had a choice about it, and He chose to give you life. He is the Creator of everything—including you. This journey is yours to travel—but God gave it to you. Never forget: God put you on the journey of life.

We came from Him—and our greatest joy will come from giving ourselves back to Him, and learning to walk with Him every day until we return to Him.

"You shall love the LORD your God
with all your heart, with all your soul,
with all your strength, and with all your mind,
and your neighbor as yourself."

LUKE 10:27

Happy are the people
whose God is the LORD!

PSALM 144:15

"I have come
that they may have life, and that they
may have it more abundantly."

JOHN 10:10

Spiritually Nourished

Many people go through life without ever realizing who they really are, or why God put them here. On the outside they may be successful, well-liked, even envied by others. But down inside something is still missing.

Advertisers promise happiness and fulfillment—if we will only use their product. Pundits and politicians promise abundance and world peace—if we will only listen to their wisdom or vote for them. These promises, however, always fall short. We spend all our time and energy pampering our bodies and minds—but if we ignore our souls, we will end up spiritually starved and malnourished. Don't let this happen to you!

The LORD will perfect
that which concerns me.

PSALM 138:8

The LORD takes pleasure in
those who fear Him,
in those who hope in His mercy.

PSALM 147:11

No longer do I call you servants, . . .
but I have called you friends,
for all things that I heard from My Father
I have made known to you.

JOHN 15:15

Put Here by God

God created us to be His friends. This was the divine plan right from the beginning, when Adam and Eve were first created—and it had its origin in the love of God.

It was, however, a friendship with a difference. On a human level we usually choose friends who are similar to us—those with like interests or a kindred personality. But God and Adam were not equals. God was the Creator; Adam was the creature. God was limitless; Adam was limited. God was independent; Adam was dependent. But in spite of the vast difference between them, God still wanted Adam and Eve to be His friends.

God's plan for Adam and Eve is also true for us. God has not changed—and neither has His purpose. We are not here by accident; we are here because God put us here—and He put us here so we could be His friends forever. Think if it: God *wants* you to be His friend!

*"Eye has not seen,
nor ear heard, nor have entered
into the heart of man the things which God has
prepared for those who love Him."*

1 CORINTHIANS 2:9

*Those who live according to the flesh set their
minds on the things of the flesh,
but those who live according to the Spirit,
the things of the Spirit.*

ROMANS 8:5

*"This is eternal life,
that they may know you,
the only true God,
and Jesus Christ whom you have sent."*

JOHN 17:3

The Great Designer

God deliberately created Adam and Eve to be His friends forever. Their fellowship with God was an unbroken reality every moment of the day.

You see, Adam and Eve weren't simply physical creatures, they were also spiritual beings, created with a soul or spirit that gave them the ability to know and experience God. In fact, the Bible says they were made in God's image—that is, God implanted something of Himself inside of them: "God created man in his own image, in the image of God he created him; male and female he created them" (Genesis 1:27 NIV). God gave them a unique spiritual nature. This was the Great Design of the Great Designer.

This is also true of us. Like Adam and Eve, we not only have a body and a mind, but we also have what the Bible calls a spirit or a soul. God gave it to you; He implanted part of Himself within you. Our souls set us apart from every other living creature, and that makes us unique. It also makes us fully human. Because of this, we can experience God and have fellowship with Him.

A man who has friends
must himself be friendly,
but there is a friend
who sticks closer than a brother.

PROVERBS 18:24

God demonstrates His own love
toward us, in that while we were still sinners,
Christ died for us.

ROMANS 5:8

If anyone is in Christ, he is a new creation,
old things have passed away;
behold, all things have become new.

2 CORINTHIANS 5:17

A Friend of God

Some years ago my wife and I were invited to have lunch with one of the wealthiest men in the world. He was 75 years old, and as he sat at the dining table tears came down his cheeks. "I am the most miserable man in the world," he said. "I have everything anyone could ever want. If I want to go anywhere, I have my own yacht or private plane. If I want something, I can buy it, no matter what it costs. But down inside I'm miserable and empty."

Shortly after visiting that man, Ruth and I met another man who preached in a small church nearby. He was vivacious and full of life, and he told us, "I don't have a penny to my name, but I'm the happiest man in the world!" The empty space in his soul had been filled. He had become the friend of God—and that made all the difference.

You, O Lord, are a shield for me,
my glory and the One who lifts up my head.

PSALM 3:3

You will show me the path of life;
in Your presence is fullness of joy;
at Your right hand are pleasures forevermore.

PSALM 16:11

The path of the just is like the shining sun,
that shines ever brighter unto the perfect day.

PROVERBS 4:18

Filled with Purpose

Perhaps you see your life's journey as a series of unrelated events—some good, some bad—strung together like beads on a string. Or perhaps you feel trapped like a leaf in a rushing stream, tossed about by circumstances beyond your control. Or like many people you may never have stopped to think about the road you are traveling—never asking where you came from, or why you are here, or where you are going.

But God didn't intend for our journey through life to be this way. Instead, He meant for it to be filled with joy and purpose, with even the most ordinary events being part of His plan. He also wants to guide us as we make decisions, and give us hope for the future.

*I will instruct you and teach you
in the way you should go;
I will guide you with My eye.*

PSALM 32:8

*You are my rock and my fortress;
therefore, for Your name's sake,
lead me and guide me.*

PSALM 31:3

*"The Dayspring from on high has visited us;
to give light to those who sit in darkness
and the shadow of death,
to guide our feet into the way of peace."*

LUKE 1:78–79

Blueprint for Living

An architect draws the plans for a new building—but it still has to be built. A composer writes a new piece of music—but it still has to be played. A chef devises a new recipe—but the ingredients still have to be cooked.

In the same way, God has given us a blueprint for living—but we must know what it is, and then put it into action. And this can happen, because God doesn't leave us to do it alone. He wants to be with us every step of the way, guiding and helping us (and even correcting us when necessary), because He loves us and wants what is best for us.

Make it your goal to seek His blueprint for your life—and then to follow it.

*Those who are wise shall shine
like the brightness of the firmament,
and those who turn many to righteousness
like the stars forever and ever.*

DANIEL 12:3

*Do not be conformed to this world,
but be transformed by the renewing of your mind,
that you may prove what is that
good and acceptable and perfect will of God.*

ROMANS 12:2

A God-Given Purpose

Some people are focused, using all their energies to reach their goals. Others drift through life with little purpose or direction, living for the moment and never thinking about where they are headed. Most people probably live somewhere in between. But they all have this in common: They are living only for themselves and their own happiness.

But when we come to Christ, God gives us a new purpose. Now we want to live for Christ and not just ourselves. We begin to see other people differently—not for what they can do for us, but what we can do for them.

When I came to Christ I had little inkling of what I might do with my life, but down inside I knew something was different. Before my conversion, for example, I tended to be touchy and irritable. Now I deliberately tried to be considerate and courteous. Some may not have noticed, but my parents did—and so did I. Little by little I was beginning to have a new purpose in life: a desire to live for Christ. I was learning that "those who live should no longer live for themselves but for him who died for them and was raised again" (2 Corinthians 5:15 NIV).

Teach me Your way, O LORD,
and lead me in a smooth path.

PSALM 27:11

Make me walk in the
path of Your commandments,
for I delight in it.

PSALM 119:35

Ponder the path of your feet,
and let all your ways be established.

PROVERBS 4:26

The Right Path

Can our lives be different? Can we know for sure that we will go to Heaven when we die? The answer is yes—and the reason is because of what Jesus Christ did for us. We can have our sins forgiven, and we can begin life again by God's grace. Our journey through life can be different by traveling a new path—God's path.

Even before time began, God knew all about us and planned this new path for us. He looked across the ages and saw that we would be helpless and lost in sin, unable to find the right road on our own. He saw *you*. From all eternity He planned to provide another way—a way that will take us to Heaven some day, and gives us purpose and peace in the meantime. That way is Jesus, who alone could say, "I am the way and the truth and the life. No one comes to the Father except through me" (John 14:6 NIV).

Sin has put us firmly on the wrong path. But because of Jesus, we can be firmly on the right path—and that's what we need.

"Come to Me,
all you who labor and are heavy laden,
and I will give you rest."

MATTHEW 11:28

Ask for the old paths,
where the good way is,
and walk in it.

JEREMIAH 6:16

I have chosen the way of truth.

PSALM 119:30

Avoiding Life's Pitfalls

Are we destined to lurch down life's road from one pothole or detour to another?

Down inside we all sense that this was not the way life was meant to be, and we yearn for something better. We suspect there must be another way, a different path from the one we have been traveling. But why do so few people seem to find it? Why have we missed it? Can life be any different?

The answer to that last question is Yes! No matter who you are or what your life has been like so far, the rest of your life's journey can be different. With God's help you can begin again. With Him you can confront your problems and begin to deal with them, and you can avoid life's pitfalls and detours. More than that, with God's help you can make an impact on our world. If you have never done so, ask Jesus Christ into your life today.

*You shall go out with joy,
and be led out with peace; the mountains
and the hills shall break forth
into singing before you, and all the trees
of the field shall clap their hands.*

ISAIAH 55:12

*May the God of hope fill you with all
joy and peace in believing,
that you may abound in hope by the
power of the Holy Spirit.*

ROMANS 15:13

*He shall pray to God,
and He will delight in him, He shall
see His face with joy, for He restores
to man His righteousness.*

JOB 33:26

Joy and Peace

Whatever has happened in your life so far—both good and bad—cannot be altered, and all the decisions and events that have made you what you are today are indelibly inscribed in the story of your life.

But with God's help you *can* change the future. The future doesn't need to be a copy of the past, nor does God want it to be. No matter what your life has been like so far, God wants to put your feet on a new path . . . a better path . . . His path. And regardless of what you may have thought, His path promises joy and peace and purpose far beyond anything you could have imagined. Which path are you on today—your path, or God's path?

Confident in
God's Love

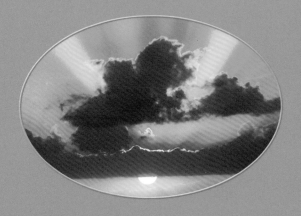

*The love of God has been
poured out in our hearts by the Holy Spirit
who was given to us.*

ROMANS 5:5

No one is holy like the LORD,
for there is none besides You,
nor is there any rock like our God.

1 SAMUEL 2:2

Who is God, except the LORD?
And who is a rock, except our God?

PSALM 18:31

O LORD God of hosts, who is
mighty like You, O LORD? Your faithfulness
also surrounds You.

PSALM 89:8

The solid foundation of God stands,
having this seal:
"The Lord knows those who are His."

2 TIMOTHY 2:19

God—Our Mighty Rock

Just as a careful builder first lays a solid foundation before constructing a building, so God's Word gives us a solid foundation for building our spiritual lives. The Bible says, "For no one can lay any foundation other than the one already laid, which is Jesus Christ" (1 Corinthians 3:11 NIV).

Why is this important? Because if we aren't sure whether or not God loves us, our journey through life will be hesitant, uncertain, insecure. But if we have confidence in God's love, then our journey will be joyful, assured and filled with hope. A true Christian isn't prideful or arrogant; his confidence is not in himself but in God, and he humbly trusts Him every day. With the Psalmist he says, "My salvation and my honor depend on God; he is my mighty rock, my refuge" (Psalm 62:7 NIV). Is Christ the foundation of your life?

*What manner of love the Father
has bestowed on us,
that we should be called children of God!*

1 JOHN 3:1

*In Him you also trusted, after you heard
the word of truth, the gospel of your salvation;
in whom also, having believed,
you were sealed with the Holy Spirit of promise.*

EPHESIANS 1:13

*The grace of God that brings salvation
has appeared to all men.*

TITUS 2:11

God Is Gracious

One reason many Christians aren't sure of their salvation is because they still sin, and they fear God may reject them because of it. "God must be very disappointed in me," one man wrote me. "I don't see how I can still be a Christian when I keep losing my temper."

Sin is serious. But even when we sin, the Bible says, "The LORD is gracious and compassionate, slow to anger and rich in love" (Psalm 145:8 NIV).

Suppose someone gave you a computer for your birthday. "This is my gift to you," they said, and you thanked them for being so generous. But suppose they added, "However, I have one requirement. Although I know you've never had a computer before, if you make a mistake on it—even one—then I'm going to take it back. You can't keep this computer unless you're perfect!" What would you think?

Yet many people assume God is like that: giving us the gift of salvation—then taking it back if we aren't perfect! But it isn't true.

Having been justified by faith,
we have peace with God
through our Lord Jesus Christ.

ROMANS 5:1

A man is not justified
by the works of the law but by
faith in Jesus Christ.

GALATIANS 2:16

God so loved the world that
He gave His only begotten Son,
that whoever believes in Him should not
perish but have everlasting life.

JOHN 3:16

Confident in Christ Alone

G od doesn't save us because of who we are or how good we are, nor can we ever claim we are better than others—because we aren't. God has saved us solely by His mercy and grace, and we can't take any credit for our salvation—none at all. The Bible says, "For it is by grace you have been saved, through faith— and this not from yourselves, it is the gift of God—not by works, so that no one can boast" (Ephesians 2:8–9 NIV). God's grace—His goodness and love toward us in spite of our sin—is the wellspring of our salvation.

Our confidence must be in Christ, and Christ alone. The Bible says, "God has given us eternal life, and this life is in his Son. He who has the Son has life; he who does not have the Son of God does not have life" (1 John 5:11–12 NIV).

*Christ . . . has sealed us and
given us the Spirit in our hearts as a guarantee.*

2 CORINTHIANS 1:22

*Our gospel did not come to you in word only,
but also in power, and in
the Holy Spirit and in much assurance.*

1 THESSALONIANS 1:5

*The work of righteousness will
be peace, and the effect of righteousness,
quietness and assurance forever.*

ISAIAH 32:17

A Settled Assurance

God has given us an inner witness to assure us of our salvation: the witness of the Holy Spirit. This witness within us isn't just an emotional feeling (although emotions may play a part). Instead, the Spirit's witness is a settled, inner conviction that the Gospel is true, and we now belong to Christ.

This is somewhat like being a member of a family. Sometimes you may feel very close to your family; sometimes you may not. But down inside you always know you are part of that family, whether you feel close to them or not. You know you belong to each other; you have a settled, inner conviction that isn't just an emotional feeling. In fact, it isn't based on your feelings at all. It is based on a fact—the fact that you were born into that family. In the same way, the Holy Spirit gives us an inner, settled conviction that we have been born into a family—the family of God, who is our Heavenly Father.

You shall receive power when
the Holy Spirit has come upon you. . . .

ACTS 1:8

Do you not know that your body
is the temple of the Holy Spirit who is
in you, whom you have from God,
and you are not your own?

1 CORINTHIANS 6:19

The Helper, the Holy Spirit,
whom the Father will send in My name,
He will teach you all things, and bring to your
remembrance all things that I said to you.

JOHN 14:26

God Is with Us

When we come to Christ, God Himself comes to live within us by His Holy Spirit. We are not alone; God is with us!

If you know Christ, you don't need to beg for the Holy Spirit to come into your life; He is already there—whether you "feel" His presence or not. Don't confuse the Holy Spirit with an emotional feeling, or a particular type of spiritual experience. Instead, accept by faith what God promised: When you come to Christ, the Holy Spirit comes to live within you.

Why has God given us the Holy Spirit? The Spirit has been given for many reasons—but one is to help us live the way we should. God has given us a new purpose—but without a new power we'll never be able to achieve it. We are too weak! But the Bible says, "the Spirit helps us in our weakness" (Romans 8:26 NIV). We aren't meant to live the Christian life in our own strength. God has provided His Spirit to help us.

He has appeared to put away sin
by the sacrifice of Himself.

HEBREWS 9:26

Not with the blood of goats and calves,
but with His own blood
He entered the Most Holy Place once for all,
having obtained eternal redemption.

HEBREWS 9:12

If we walk in the light as He is in the light,
we have fellowship with one another,
and the blood of Jesus Christ His Son
cleanses us from all sin.

1 JOHN 1:7

A Complete Sacrifice

Y ou and I can't add anything to what Christ did for us, because He has done it all. If Christ's death was not enough . . . if we needed to add our own good works to His in order to be saved . . . then we could never know for sure that we will go to Heaven when we die, because we could never be sure if we have done enough. But the ransom has been fully paid, and Christ's work is finished.

Nothing more remains to be done. Christ's sacrifice is complete! His work on your behalf is finished! Pause right now and thank Him for making you part of His family forever.

*His divine power has given to us all things
that pertain to life and godliness, through the knowledge
of Him who called us by glory and virtue.*

2 PETER 1:3

*I pray . . . that they also may be one in Us,
that the world may believe that You sent Me. And the
glory which You gave Me I have given them,
that they may be one just as We are one.*

JOHN 17:21–22

*All of you be of one mind,
having compassion for one another; love as brothers,
be tenderhearted, be courteous.*

1 PETER 3:8

A Family Resemblance

G od's will is for us to become more and more like Christ. It is that simple—and also that complex.

Perhaps you've had the experience of having someone come up to you and say, "You look just like your mother!" or "You look just like your brother!" They saw a family resemblance between you and your parents or some other member of your family. Grandparents often spend hours trying to decide who a newborn baby resembles in the family (usually with little success!). You may even have seen married couples who looked more and more like each other as the years went by.

In a far deeper way, God's will is that we would bear a family resemblance to His Son. In other words, God's plan is for us to become more and more like Jesus— not physically, of course, but in the way we think and act and treat other people. Is this your goal?

*"If anyone desires to come after Me,
let him deny himself,
and take up his cross daily, and follow Me."*

LUKE 9:23

"He must increase, but I must decrease."

JOHN 3:30

*I also count all things loss
for the excellence of the knowledge
of Christ Jesus my Lord.*

PHILIPPIANS 3:8

Lord of All

God's will is for you to become more and more like Christ right where you are. Jesus didn't isolate Himself from daily life; He became involved in people's lives wherever He went. At times He withdrew to rest and spend time alone with His Heavenly Father—and so should we. But Jesus also knew what it was to live under pressure, and yet He never wavered from God's plan for His life. Neither should we.

How do we become more like Christ? How does it happen? It happens as we submit every area of our lives to His authority. Nothing must be excluded from His influence, and nothing must be withheld from His control. Many years ago I heard someone use a little phrase I have never forgotten: "If Christ is to be Lord *at* all, then He must be Lord *of* all."

*"These things I have spoken to you,
that My joy may remain in you, and that
your joy may be full."*

JOHN 15:11

*May the God of patience and comfort
grant you to be like-minded toward one another,
according to Christ Jesus, that you may
with one mind and one mouth glorify the God
and Father of our Lord Jesus Christ.*

ROMANS 15:5

*You were bought at a price;
therefore glorify God in your body and
in your spirit, which are God's.*

1 CORINTHIANS 6:20

Pleasing and Perfect

People saw in Jesus a quality of life they had never seen before, and they wanted to experience it for themselves. When they looked at Him they saw joy and peace and kindness—and most of all, they saw God's love.

God wants to give us that same quality of life—the life of Jesus. Jesus said to His disciples, "I have told you this so that my joy may be in you and that your joy may be complete" (John 15:11 NIV).

God's plan is to remake us from within, by His Holy Spirit. The Bible says, "Do not conform any longer to the pattern of this world, but be transformed by the renewing of your mind. Then you will be able to test and approve what God's will is—his good, pleasing and perfect will" (Romans 12:2 NIV).

That's what God's will is like: good, pleasing and perfect. Why settle for anything less?

Growing in God's Love

He will love you and bless you
and multiply you.

DEUTERONOMY 7:13

*"I will pray the Father, and He will
give you another Helper, that He may abide with
you forever—the Spirit of truth."*

John 14:16–17

*As many as are led by the Spirit of God,
these are sons of God.*

Romans 8:14

*Thanks be to God who always leads us
in triumph in Christ, and through us diffuses the
fragrance of His knowledge in every place.*

2 Corinthians 2:14

We Need God's Power

As humans we have two great spiritual needs. The first is forgiveness, which God made possible by sending His Son into the world to die for our sins. Our second need, however, is for goodness, which God also made possible by sending the Holy Spirit to dwell within us.

If we are to live the way God meant us to live . . . if we are to become more like Christ . . . if we are to travel our journey wisely . . . then we need *both* God's forgiveness and goodness. We need the work of the Son *for* us, and we need the work of the Holy Spirit *in* us. To the great gift of forgiveness God adds the great gift of the Holy Spirit. As a friend of mine once said, "I need Jesus Christ for my eternal life, and the Holy Spirit of God for my internal life."

*The Spirit Himself bears witness
with our spirit that we are children of God.*

ROMANS 8:16

*He who . . . has anointed us is God,
who also has sealed us and given us the Spirit in
our hearts as a guarantee.*

2 CORINTHIANS 1:21–22

*"When He, the Spirit of truth, has come,
He will guide you into all truth."*

JOHN 16:13

Changed by God's Spirit

Many Christians know they should be better persons, and they struggle with all their might to change their behavior. But most of their attempts at self improvement fail, and they end up frustrated and discouraged. They can echo the words of the Apostle Paul: "I have the desire to do what is good, but I cannot carry it out. For what I do is not the good I want to do; no, the evil I do not want to do—this I keep on doing" (Romans 7:18–19 NIV).

What is the problem? The problem is that we are relying on our own strength instead of the strength of the Holy Spirit. We not only need to know how God wants us to live; we also need the power to achieve it. And God has given us that power by giving us His Holy Spirit. He gives us the Bible to teach us, and other Christians to encourage us—but He also gives us His Spirit to change us. Not only do we have other Christians around us, but we have the Holy Spirit within us. He is our constant, unchanging companion on the journey.

*"Whoever drinks of the water that I shall
give him will never thirst. But the water that
I shall give him will become in him a fountain of
water springing up into everlasting life."*

JOHN 4:14

*"I am the Alpha and the Omega,
the Beginning and the End.
I will give of the fountain of the water
of life freely to him who thirsts."*

REVELATION 21:6

*O God, You are my God;
early will I seek You; My soul thirsts
for You; My flesh longs for You in a
dry and thirsty land.*

PSALM 63:1

Life-Giving Water

The water for our home in the mountains of North Carolina comes from a spring above the house. When we moved there the old-timers in the area told us this particular spring would always flow, even in the worst drought—and they were right. One year, however, we had an abnormally cold winter, and one day we found ourselves without water. Ice had formed in the pipe running from the spring, and we had to dig through the frozen ground and use a blowtorch to melt it. Only then did the flow resume.

I have often compared that spring to the Holy Spirit. No matter the circumstances, the Holy Spirit's flow is always available to us—just like that spring. But sin is like the ice that blocked our pipe. We allow the spiritual coldness of a hostile world to freeze our souls and cut off the Spirit's life-giving water.

The only way to clear the blockage and restore the flow is through repentance. If your spiritual life is dry and barren, begin by praying the Psalmist's prayer: "Search me, O God, and know my heart. . . . See if there is any offensive way in me" (Psalm 139:23–24 NIV).

I have restrained my feet
from every evil way
that I may keep Your word.

PSALM 119:101

"I have been crucified with Christ;
it is no longer I who live,
but Christ lives in me; and the life
which I now live in the flesh
I live by faith in the Son of God,
who loved me and gave Himself for me."

GALATIANS 2:20

Draw near to God
and He will draw near to you.

JAMES 4:8

A New Start Each Day

Being filled with the Holy Spirit isn't a once-for-all event, but a continuous reality every day of our lives. Is it for you?

Personally I find it helpful to begin each day by silently committing it to God (even before I get up), thanking Him that I belong to Him, and that He knows what the day holds for me. Then I ask Him to use me that day for His glory, and to cleanse me from every sin that might hinder this.

Then I step out in faith, believing His Spirit will fill me as I obey His Word and trust in Him. I won't always be aware of His presence, but at the end of the day I know I'll be able to look back and thank Him for being with me and guiding me. He promised to be with me that day—and He was.

This can be your experience also, as you yield your life daily to Christ's Lordship. Give each day to Him, so that at its end you can look back and thank Him for being with you, as He promised.

Be anxious for nothing,
but in everything by prayer and supplication,
with thanksgiving, let your requests be
made known to God; and the peace of God,
which surpasses all understanding, will guard your
hearts and minds through Christ Jesus.

PHILIPPIANS 4:6–7

The eyes of the LORD are on the righteous,
and His ears are open to their cry.

PSALM 34:15

Rejoice always, pray without ceasing,
in everything give thanks; for this
is the will of God in Christ Jesus for you.

1 THESSALONIANS 5:16–18

God Cares

One of God's most comforting promises is that we can bring every need and burden to Him: "Cast your cares on the LORD and he will sustain you; he will never let the righteous fall" (Psalm 55:22 NIV). The Bible also says, "The prayer of a righteous man is powerful and effective" (James 5:16 NIV). One of my strongest memories of our trips to Africa and India was the prayer meetings we attended—sometimes with thousands gathered in the early morning. I have seldom heard such fervent prayer, and the reason was because they deeply believed prayer is "powerful and effective." God's Word is filled with promises about prayer, and repeatedly He tells us to bring our burdens to Him.

In fact, God urges us to bring our concerns to Him—not just petitions about our own needs, but also intercessions for others. Just as an earthly father wants his children to come to him with their requests, so our Heavenly Father wants us to come to Him.

*Be sober, be vigilant; because your
adversary the devil walks about like a roaring lion,
seeking whom he may devour.*

1 PETER 5:8

*Each one is tempted when he is
drawn away by his own desires and enticed.*

JAMES 1:14

*Put on the Lord Jesus Christ,
and make no provision for the flesh,
to fulfill its lusts.*

ROMANS 13:14

*Put on the whole armor of God,
that you may be able to
stand against the wiles of the devil.*

EPHESIANS 6:11

Strength to Face Temptation

Temptation isn't the same thing as sin, and it isn't a sin to be tempted. Temptation is being enticed to do wrong; sin is actually doing it. It isn't a sin to be tempted, but it is a sin to give in to the temptation. At the beginning of His ministry "Jesus was led by the Spirit into the desert to be tempted by the devil" (Matthew 4:1 NIV). But Jesus didn't give in to Satan's temptations (although they were very intense and alluring). The Bible says Jesus was "tempted in every way, just as we are—yet was without sin" (Hebrews 4:15 NIV).

Whenever I am tempted to do something wrong I gain great strength from those words about Jesus. You and I will never face a temptation He doesn't understand, for He was tempted "in every way, just as we are." He knows what we are going through when we are tempted, because He has already been there. But He also points the way to victory, because He faced temptation's challenge—and overcame it. So can we.

Search me, O God, and know my heart.

PSALM 139:23

"Watch and pray,
lest you enter into temptation.
The spirit indeed is willing,
but the flesh is weak."

MATTHEW 26:41

The Spirit also helps us in our weaknesses.

ROMANS 8:26

Blessed is the man who endures temptation;
for when he has been approved,
he will receive the crown of life which the Lord
has promised to those who love Him.

JAMES 1:12

A Clear Distinction

We need to know what the Bible teaches about right and wrong. Every day we are battered by messages—from the media, advertising, entertainment, celebrities, even our friends—with one underlying message: "Live for yourself." The world hammers away at us, trying to shape us into its mold and make us believe that sin isn't really sin. After all, isn't everyone doing it? But God says, "Do not conform any longer to the pattern of this world, but be transformed by the renewing of your mind" (Romans 12:2 NIV).

Ask God to help you recognize temptation when it comes. When you are unsure whether or not something is wrong, ask yourself these questions: Does this glorify God? Does it draw me closer to Christ, or does it make me preoccupied with this world? Will it harm my health, or hurt me in some other way? Will it cause someone else to stumble spiritually or morally (especially a less mature Christian)? I have never forgotten what a wise Christian said to me many years ago: "When in doubt—don't!"

Great peace have those who love Your law,
and nothing causes them to stumble.

PSALM 119:165

All Scripture is given by inspiration of God,
and is profitable for doctrine,
for reproof, for correction, for instruction
in righteousness, that the man
of God may be complete,
thoroughly equipped for every good work.

2 TIMOTHY 3:16–17

Be doers of the word, and not hearers only.

JAMES 1:22

God's "Love Letter"

The Bible isn't just for preachers and scholars! God wants to speak to you through His Word, and no matter who you are, the Bible can come alive to you. You may never understand *everything* in the Bible, but you can understand *something*.

Bible reading shouldn't be a burden but a joy! I vividly remember the day I received Ruth's letter saying she had decided to accept my proposal for marriage. I probably read and reread it dozens of times that day! God wants to talk with us through His Word—in fact, it is His "love letter" to us. Why shouldn't we come to it joyfully?

Ask God to speak to you through its pages—and then expect Him to do so. This doesn't mean every time we open the Bible we'll find something new; God may be underlining truths we already know. But let the Psalmist's prayer become yours: "Open my eyes that I may see wonderful things in your law" (Psalm 119:18 NIV).

As for God, His way is perfect;
the word of the LORD is proven;
He is a shield to all who trust in Him.

PSALM 18:30

"I am the LORD, I do not change."

MALACHI 3:6

His divine power has given to us all things
that pertain to life and godliness,
through the knowledge of Him
who called us by glory and virtue,
by which have been given to us exceedingly
great and precious promises.

2 PETER 1:3−4

You are good, and do good;
teach me Your statutes.

PSALM 119:68

God's Dependable Word

From time to time children write me with their questions about God. One favorite question is this: Is there anything God can't do? I always answer "yes." The one thing God can't do, I explain, is anything wrong. For example, I add, God can never tell a lie—and because of that, we can trust whatever He promises us in His Word, the Bible.

From one end of the Bible to the other God assures us that He will never go back on His promises. Make them the foundation of your life every day.

I love the LORD,
because He has heard my voice.

PSALM 116:1

Certainly God has heard me;
He has attended to the voice of my prayer.

PSALM 66:19

Trust in Him at all times, you people;
pour out your heart before Him;
God is a refuge for us.

PSALM 62:8

God looks down from heaven
upon the children of men, to see if there are any
who understand, who seek God.

PSALM 53:2

The Gift of Prayer

Central to any relationship is communication. It's true on a human level; what kind of relationship do two people have who never talk with each other? In a far greater way, our relationship with God involves communication—not just an occasional brief chat, but a deep sharing of ourselves and our concerns with God. Because Christ has opened Heaven's door for us, the Bible says, we should "approach the throne of grace with confidence, so that we may receive mercy and find grace to help us in our time of need" (Hebrews 4:16 NIV).

In the Bible God speaks to us; in prayer we speak to God. Both are essential—and both are gifts God has given us so we can know each other. Prayer is a gift from God's hand just as much as the Bible, and He has given us the privilege of prayer because He loves us and wants our fellowship.

Hear my cry, O God;
attend to my prayer.

PSALM 61:1

Cast your burden on the LORD,
and He shall sustain you;
He will never permit
the righteous to be moved.

PSALM 55:22

The effective, fervent prayer
of a righteous man avails much.

JAMES 5:16

A Person of Prayer

Every man or woman whose life has ever counted for God has been a person of prayer.

Jesus demonstrated the importance of prayer by His own example. His whole ministry was saturated with prayer. On one occasion, "Very early in the morning, while it was still dark, Jesus got up, left the house and went off to a solitary place, where he prayed" (Mark 1:35 NIV). On another occasion "Jesus was praying in a certain place. When he finished, one of his disciples said to him, 'Lord, teach us to pray'" (Luke 11:1 NIV). He responded by giving them what came to be His most-quoted words, the Lord's Prayer. As His death approached He withdrew to the Garden of Gethsemane, a secluded place outside the walls of Jerusalem, to pray, "And being in anguish, he prayed more earnestly, and his sweat was like drops of blood falling to the ground" (Luke 22:44 NIV). His last words from the cross were a prayer: "Father, into your hands I commit my spirit" (Luke 23:46 NIV). If prayer was this important to the Son of God during His journey on earth, shouldn't it be important to us?

Ask, and it will be given to you;
seek, and you will find;
knock, and it will be opened to you.

MATTHEW 7:7

"Your will be done on earth
as it is in heaven."

MATTHEW 6:10

"We have no power against this
great multitude that is coming against us;
nor do we know what to do, but our
eyes are upon You."

2 CHRONICLES 20:12

A Declaration of Dependence

A friend of mine likes to define prayer as "a declaration of dependence"—and he has a point. We will only pray when we realize how dependent we are on God, and we trust Him to hear our prayers and answer them according to His will. Recently I saw a documentary on television about the bombing of London during the Second World War. One man in the program said that when the bombs began to fall he began praying for the first time in his life. I'm sure the same is true for countless people who never think about God, but suddenly find themselves in a crisis that is beyond them and cry out for help. They are realizing—even if dimly—that they are dependent on God after all.

God wants us to bring our every concern to Him in prayer, and to be persistent in our praying.

My heart is steadfast,
O God, my heart is steadfast;
I will sing and give praise.

PSALM 57:7

In everything give thanks; for this is
the will of God in Christ Jesus for you.

1 THESSALONIANS 5:18

Blessed be the God and Father
of our Lord Jesus Christ, who has
blessed us with every spiritual blessing
in the heavenly places in Christ.

EPHESIANS 1:3

Praise the LORD! For it is good
to sing praises to our God; for it is pleasant,
and praise is beautiful.

PSALM 147:1

Giving Thanks to God

When we praise God, our focus is on Him, not on ourselves. Many of the Psalms are actually prayers, and it is no accident that the word "praise" occurs in the book of Psalms over one hundred times.

The Bible says, "Enter his gates with thanksgiving and his courts with praise; give thanks to him and praise his name" (Psalm 100:4 NIV).

Why should we give thanks? One reason is because everything we have comes from God: "Every good and perfect gift is from above, coming down from the Father" (James 1:17 NIV). We can't take credit for anything—even our successes. God gave us our abilities; He arranged our circumstances; He blessed our efforts. Therefore, the Bible says, "Give thanks to the LORD, for he is good; his love endures forever" (Psalm 106:1 NIV). Make thankfulness a part of your life, today and always.

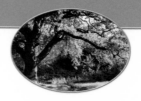

*The LORD is near to all who call upon Him,
to all who call upon Him in truth.*

PSALM 145:18

*While I live I will praise the LORD;
I will sing praises to my God while
I have my being.*

PSALM 146:2

*Let the hearts of those
rejoice who seek the Lord!
Seek the LORD and His strength;
seek His face evermore!*

PSALM 105:3–4

*I will bless the LORD at all times;
His praise shall continually be in my mouth.*

PSALM 34:1

Prayer and Praise

If all we do is ask God for things we want, our prayers quickly become selfish. Although the thought might shock us, we begin to think of God as little more than a glorified Santa Claus to whom we turn only when we want something. But God is far greater than this. Remember: God isn't our servant; we are His servants.

True prayer begins by seeing God as He really is—and that is why praise should be a regular part of our prayers. When we praise God, our focus is on Him, not on ourselves.

You are a child of God if you know Christ, and He welcomes your prayers. He is much more concerned about our hearts than our eloquence.

Let us not give up meeting together,
as some are in the habit of doing,
but let us encourage one another—
and all the more as you see the
Day [of Christ's return] approaching.

HEBREWS 10:25 NIV

The things you have heard from me
among many witnesses,
commit these to faithful men
who will be able to teach others also.

2 TIMOTHY 2:2

Be filled with the Spirit,
speaking to one another in psalms
and hymns and spiritual songs, singing and
making melody in your heart to the Lord.

EPHESIANS 5:18–19

Part of God's Family

We not only belong to God, we also belong to each other.

We aren't traveling alone on this journey God has given; others are traveling it with us. But unlike a race or a marathon, we aren't competing with each other or trying to get ahead of them and win. We are traveling together on this journey, sharing its joys and bearing each other's burdens and heartaches. If someone stumbles, we help them get to their feet; if someone veers off course, we urge them back. On this journey we are all brothers and sisters in the same family—the family of God.

This family is what the New Testament calls the Church. In its fullest sense "the Church" isn't just a particular building or congregation, but the spiritual fellowship of all who belong to Jesus Christ. If we belong to Christ, we also belong to each other; if we have committed our lives to Him, we are also committed to each other. The reason is simple: We need each other.

The hour is coming, and now is,
when the true worshipers will worship
the Father in spirit and truth;
for the Father is seeking such
to worship Him.

JOHN 4:23

Be kind to one another, tenderhearted,
forgiving one another,
even as God in Christ forgave you.

EPHESIANS 4:32

Let the word of Christ dwell in you richly
in all wisdom, teaching and
admonishing one another in psalms
and hymns and spiritual songs,
singing with grace in your hearts to the Lord.

COLOSSIANS 3:16

The Gift of Each Other

The word *Church* in the Bible refers to the company of all believers, who are spiritually united by their relationship with Christ. The Church isn't just a local congregation; it includes all believers everywhere—even those who have died and are now in Heaven. As my mother approached death she wasn't only looking forward to being with Christ, but being reunited with friends and family who had already entered Heaven. If you belong to Christ, you are part of this great invisible fellowship of believers across the ages. The Bible tells us that "Christ is the head of the church, his body, of which he is the Savior" (Ephesians 5:23 NIV).

The Bible is God's gift to you—but your fellow Christians are His gift to you also. God has given us to each other. One of the main tools God uses to shape us and make us more like Christ is our fellowship with other Christians. In fact, unless we have active contact with other believers our spiritual lives will be stunted. The Bible says, "As iron sharpens iron, so one man sharpens another" (Proverbs 27:17 NIV). Our fellowship with other believers is a gift from God.

*Since we are receiving a kingdom
which cannot be shaken, let us have grace,
by which we may serve God acceptably
with reverence and godly fear.*

HEBREWS 12:28

*Comfort each other and edify one another,
just as you also are doing.*

1 THESSALONIANS 5:11

*[Christ] we preach,
warning every man and teaching
every man in all wisdom, that we may present
every man perfect in Christ Jesus.*

COLOSSIANS 1:28

Encouragement and Wisdom

We need each other's encouragement and wisdom. Sometimes we may encourage someone without even being aware of it. I can't begin to count the times I have heard a preacher or Bible teacher and said to myself afterward, "That message was exactly what I needed!" Even your example of attending church may encourage someone who is searching for God, although you may never know it.

We also encourage each other on a personal level. Some of my greatest encouragement over the years has come from godly friends who were willing to pray and share their wisdom with me. Whenever we are with other believers—whether in a church service with hundreds of people or just sharing a cup of coffee with a Christian friend—God can lift us up and increase our faith through their encouragement and counsel.

Living in
God's Love

He will quiet you with His love,
He will rejoice over you with singing.

Zephaniah 3:17

We . . . do not cease to pray for you,
and to ask that you may be filled with
the knowledge of His will
in all wisdom and spiritual understanding.

COLOSSIANS 1:9

Be renewed in the spirit of your mind,
and . . . put on the new man which
was created according to God,
in true righteousness and holiness.

EPHESIANS 4:23–24

Just as Christ was raised from the dead
by the glory of the Father, even so
we also should walk in newness of life.

ROMANS 6:4

A Whole New Life

When we come to Christ, God gives us a whole new life: a new relationship, a new citizenship, a new family, a new purpose, a new power, a new destiny.

But this isn't the end of His bounty, for God also gives us one final gift: a new journey—a whole new path to follow until the day He takes us to Heaven.

Coming to Christ isn't an end but a beginning—the beginning of a whole new life. We aren't only called to *become* Christians; we are also called to *be* Christians. Don't ever think that faith in Christ is just a type of "spiritual life insurance"—something we obtain and then put away until we need it to get into Heaven. The Christian life is a new journey—one that will take us the rest of our lives.

And the best part is this: We never walk it alone, for Christ walks with us.

*I can do all things
through Christ who strengthens me.*

PHILIPPIANS 4:13

*My God shall supply all your need
according to His riches in glory by Christ Jesus.*

PHILIPPIANS 4:19

*Forgetting those things which
are behind and reaching forward to those
things which are ahead,
I press toward the goal for the prize
of the upward call of God in Christ Jesus.*

PHILIPPIANS 3:13–14

God's Rich Resources

Our journey—our race—lasts as long as God gives us life, and we aren't meant to wander off the track, or quit and join the spectators, or decide we'll just slow down and take it easy while others pass us by. Our example is Jesus, "who for the joy set before him endured the cross, scorning its shame, and sat down at the right hand of the throne of God" (Hebrews 12:2 NIV). He faithfully ran the race God had prepared for Him, even at the cost of His own blood.

God didn't intend for us to travel our journey in our own strength anyway, but only with the strength He supplies. I am convinced the main reason so many Christians become spiritually discouraged and defeated is because they have never discovered this truth. They assume it must be up to them to live the Christian life, and they never make use of the rich resources God has already provided to strengthen us for the journey. Like a guest who has been invited to a banquet but never sits down to the meal, they have never learned to draw their strength from God's resources. Don't let this be true of you!

The entrance of Your words gives light;
it gives understanding to the simple.

PSALM 119:130

"Take My yoke upon you and learn from Me,
for I am gentle and lowly in heart and
you will find rest for your souls."

MATTHEW 11:29

"If anyone loves Me, he will keep My word;
and My Father will love him,
and We will come to him
and make Our home with him."

JOHN 14:23

To Be a Disciple

Jesus said, "If you hold to my teaching, you are really my disciples" (John 8:31 NIV).

What is a disciple? A disciple is a learner or a student. The twelve whom Jesus called to be His closest companions were with Him day and night. They had a personal relationship with Him—walking with Him, eating with Him, sharing in His conversation, observing the way He lived, listening to Him preach to the crowds. But they weren't following Jesus just to enjoy His presence. As Jesus' disciples they had a purpose: to learn from Him—absorbing His teaching, learning from His example, even profiting from His rebukes. And this was true for all His disciples, not just the twelve. To be a disciple is to be a *learner*.

"Peace I leave with you,
My peace I give you;
not as the world gives do I give to you.
Let not your heart be troubled,
neither let it be afraid."

JOHN 14:27

Be of good comfort, be of one mind,
live in peace; and the God of love
and peace will be with you.

2 CORINTHIANS 13:11

May the God of peace Himself
sanctify you completely;
and may your whole spirit, soul, and body
be preserved blameless at the coming
of our Lord Jesus Christ.

1 THESSALONIANS 5:23

Peace with God

When we follow Christ we have peace—an inner peace that comes from a deep and abiding trust in His promises. One dimension of this is our peace with God. When warring nations sign a peace treaty, the fighting between them stops—and this is what has happened between us and God. At one time we were at war with God, but now "we have peace with God through our Lord Jesus Christ" (Romans 5:1 NIV).

In addition, when we walk with Christ we have peace in our hearts. The wars that once raged in our hearts are ended. So do our conflicts with other people, and we come to have peace with others. When we know Christ we truly have peace—peace with God, peace in our hearts, and peace with others.

This peace is real—just as real as God Himself. It is an inner peace—a peace in our souls and minds and emotions—that keeps us calm even in the midst of life's worst storms.

It is good for me to draw near to God;
*I have put my trust in the Lord G*OD*,*
that I may declare all Your works.

PSALM 73:28

Draw near to God and
He will draw near to you.
Cleanse your hands, you sinners;
and purify your hearts,
you double-minded.

JAMES 4:8

"In the world you will
have tribulation;
but be of good cheer,
I have overcome the world."

JOHN 16:33

Near to God

The key to spiritual victory is to stay close to God. The Bible puts it this way: "Submit yourselves, then, to God. Resist the devil, and he will flee from you. Come near to God and he will come near to you" (James 4:7–8 NIV). *Submit . . . resist . . . come near—* this is what we must do if we are to gain spiritual victory.

If you know Christ, you have a personal relationship with God. God isn't a remote, forbidding figure who doesn't want anything to do with you. He is your loving Heavenly Father, and even now His Son is praying for you. Therefore, the Bible says, "let us draw near to God with a sincere heart in full assurance of faith" (Hebrews 10:22 NIV). You can come near to God because He wants you to!

"If you have faith as a mustard seed,
you will say to this mountain,
'Move from here to there,' and it will move;
and nothing will be impossible for you."

MATTHEW 17:20

Watch, stand fast in the faith,
be brave, be strong.

1 CORINTHIANS 16:13

How can a young man cleanse his way?
By taking heed according to Your word. . . .
Your word I have hidden in my heart,
that I might not sin against You.

PSALM 119:9, 11

Building a Strong Faith

I f our faith isn't rooted in the Bible, it will wither like a plant pulled out of the soil. Only a strong faith—a faith based on God's Word—will protect us from temptation and doubt.

Do you want your faith to grow? Then let the Bible begin to saturate your mind and soul. One of my most enduring memories of my mother is of her sitting quietly in her favorite chair, reading her well-worn Bible every day. This was her practice right up to the end of her life, and was the reason she had such an unwavering faith. The Bible says, "faith comes from hearing the message, and the message is heard through the word of Christ" (Romans 10:17 NIV). Faith doesn't just happen; it grows when it is planted in the fertile soil of God's Word.

We have the prophetic word confirmed,
which you do well to heed as a light
that shines in a dark place.

2 PETER 1:19

Oh, how I love Your law!
It is my meditation all the day.

PSALM 119:97

The word of God is living and powerful,
and sharper than any two-edged sword,
piercing even to the division
of soul and spirit, and of joints and marrow,
and is a discerner of the thoughts
and intents of the heart.

HEBREWS 4:12

Power in God's Word

There is power in the Word of God—the power to change our lives. "'Is not my word like fire,' declares the LORD, 'and like a hammer that breaks a rock in pieces?'" (Jeremiah 23:29 NIV).

God spoke—and the heavens were formed. God spoke—and the Red Sea parted so the Israelites could escape from slavery. God spoke—and Jesus Christ rose from the dead. God spoke—and Saul, the hate-filled persecutor was converted and became Paul the apostle. Yes, there is power in the Word of God. When I quote the words of the Bible in my preaching, I know that the Holy Spirit will take those words and supernaturally use them to bring conviction and new life to others. I know too that when I prayerfully study the Bible on my own, God will use it to change me. He can do the same for you.

You who seek God,
your hearts shall live.

PSALM 69:32

Let all those who seek You rejoice
and be glad in You; and let those who
love Your salvation say continually,
"Let God be magnified!"

PSALM 70:4

Whatever things you ask in prayer,
believing, you will receive.

MATTHEW 21:22

The Practice of Prayer

I don't think I ever met a busier man than my father-in-law, Dr. L. Nelson Bell. Yet my most lasting memory of Dr. Bell is his commitment to prayer. Most mornings he would be up by 4:30 or 5:00 o'clock, alone in his study reading his well-worn Bible and spending extended time in prayer. If anyone had an excuse to bypass this it was Dr. Bell—but he saw his time alone with God as the most important event of the day. He never drew attention to it (much less bragged about it), but occasionally he would quote the Psalmist's words: "O God, thou art my God: early will I seek thee; my soul thirsteth for thee" (Psalm 63:1, KJV).

Prayer for Dr. Bell wasn't a hurried sentence or two at the end of the day or a hasty afterthought when facing a crisis. Prayer for him was a constant, moment-by-moment practice that penetrated his whole life. Prayer for him was also a joyful experience, an opportunity to come daily into God's presence. So should it be for us.

[Give] preference to one another; . . .
serving the Lord; rejoicing in hope,
patient in tribulation,
continuing steadfastly in prayer.

ROMANS 12:10–12

Continue earnestly in prayer,
being vigilant in it with thanksgiving.

COLOSSIANS 4:2

This is the confidence that we have in Him,
that if we ask anything
according to His will, He hears us.

1 JOHN 5:14

Sharing Deeply

Prayer shouldn't be a burden but a privilege—a privilege God has graciously given us because He wants our fellowship. Remember: Jesus Christ died to destroy the barrier of sin that separates us from God, and when we give our lives to Him we have a personal relationship with God. In fact, we have access to God in prayer only because of what Christ did for us by His death and resurrection.

But central to any relationship is communication. It's true on a human level; what kind of relationship do two people have who never talk with each other? In a far greater way, our relationship with God involves communication—not just an occasional brief chat, but a deep sharing of ourselves and our concerns with God.

Let my prayer be set before You
as incense, the lifting up of my hands
as the evening sacrifice.

PSALM 141:2

Hear my prayer, O LORD, give ear
to my supplications!
In Your faithfulness answer me,
and in Your righteousness.

PSALM 143:1

I will pray with the spirit,
and I will also pray
with the understanding.

1 CORINTHIANS 14:15

Everything We Need

Why do we need to pray? The reason is because the Christian life is a journey, and we need God's strength and guidance along the way. One of the major ways He supplies these is through prayer. God doesn't leave us to our own resources! Instead, He "has given us *everything we need* for life and godliness through our knowledge of him who called us by his own glory and goodness" (2 Peter 1:3 NIV, emphasis added). Prayer is part of the "everything we need" God has given us.

A prayerless Christian is a powerless Christian. A prayerless Christian is also a contradiction, because we should yearn for fellowship with the One who redeemed us. Throughout both the Bible and the history of the Church, those who made the greatest impact for God were those who prayed the most.

Guided by God's Love

We have known and believed the love
that God has for us.

1 JOHN 4:16

I have taught you in the way of wisdom;
I have led you in right paths.

PROVERBS 4:11

Your word is a lamp to my feet
and a light to my path.

PSALM 119:105

Ponder the path of your feet,
and let all your ways be established.

PROVERBS 4:26

A man's heart plans his way,
but the LORD directs his steps.

PROVERBS 16:9

Which Road?

Every time life turns against us we stand at a crossroads. When disappointment or tragedy or suffering strike, we have a decision to make: Will we turn away from God, or will we turn toward Him? Will we refuse His help, or will we seek it? Will we depend on ourselves for the strength we need, or will we depend on Him? Which road will we take? One road leads to doubt, anger, bitterness, fear, hopelessness and despair. The other leads to hope, comfort, peace, strength and joy. Which will it be?

He who heeds the word wisely
will find good, and whoever trusts
in the LORD, happy is he.

PROVERBS 16:20

If you abide in Me,
and My words abide in you,
you will ask what you desire, and it
shall be done for you.

JOHN 15:7

They seek Me daily,
and delight to know My ways. . . .
They ask of Me the ordinances of justice;
they take delight in approaching God.

ISAIAH 58:2

The Right Question

Life isn't always fair, nor is it always the way we wish it were. Disappointment, tragedy, grief, failure, disability, illness, injustice, rejection, suffering, grief—these will come our way, sometimes at the most unexpected times or in the most unexpected ways.

When they do, it's natural to ask "Why, Lord? Why did You let this happen to me?" It's not wrong to ask this; God may even answer our cry (or at least give us a hint), because He has lessons to teach us through this experience.

But the most important question we should ask when life turns against us isn't *"Why?"*, but *"What?"* "What do *You* want me to do, Lord? How should I react to this situation? What response do *You* want me to make?"

"Whoever hears these sayings of Mine,
and does them, I will liken him to a wise man
who built his house on the rock:
and the rain descended,
the floods came, and the winds blew and
beat on that house; and it did not fall,
for it was founded on the rock."

MATTHEW 7:24–25

No other foundation can anyone lay
than that which is laid, which is Jesus Christ.

1 CORINTHIANS 3:11

"Do not fear, nor be afraid;
have I not told you
from that time, and declared it?
You are My witnesses.
Is there a God besides Me? Indeed there is
no other Rock; I know not one."

ISAIAH 44:8

Strong Foundations

The time to prepare for life's disappointments and hurts is in advance, before they come crashing down upon us. *Now* is the time to build spiritual foundations that won't collapse under the weight of life's reverses.

Some months ago the remnants of a powerful hurricane tore down numerous trees around our home and caused several landslides. But the house itself was untouched, because when it was being built an architect friend advised us to set it on steel pilings driven down to solid rock, which we did.

How strong is the foundation of your life? And what are you doing to make it stronger? A house's foundation isn't built in a day, nor are our spiritual foundations. Make it your goal to build strong foundations for your life— foundations constructed from prayer and the truths of God's Word.

Blessed be the God and Father
of our Lord Jesus Christ, the Father of mercies
and God of all comfort,
who comforts us in all our tribulation.

2 CORINTHIANS 1:3–4

Neither death nor life, nor angels
nor principalities nor powers,
nor things present nor things to come,
nor height nor depth, nor any other created thing,
shall be able to separate us from the love of God
which is in Christ Jesus our Lord.

ROMANS 8:38–39

He shall cover you with His feathers,
and under His wings you shall take refuge.

PSALM 91:4

The Depth of God's Love

I still recall how stunned I felt when news came that one of my closest friends in high school had been shot down in a fighter plane over Germany. Recovering from grief, I've come to realize, isn't a single event but a process. Just as our bodies heal only gradually after major surgery, so too do our hearts after the death of someone we loved.

The Psalmist wrote, "Cast your burden on the Lord, and He shall sustain you" (Psalm 55:22). Notice that he didn't say, "Cast some of your burden on the Lord"; instead, God wants us to cast *all our burdens* on Him—including our burden of grief. Your grief over the death of someone you loved may be the biggest burden you will ever carry. Why carry it alone? Why not turn it over to God?

We will only do this when we realize two great truths: The depth of our weakness, and the depth of God's love. Don't try to carry your grief alone! Instead, turn to your loving Heavenly Father and ask Him to lift it from your shoulders—and slowly but surely He will.

Count it all joy when you fall
into various trials, knowing that
the testing of your faith produces patience.
But let patience have its perfect work,
that you may be perfect and
complete, lacking nothing.

JAMES 1:2–4

"My grace is sufficient for you,
for My strength is made perfect in weakness."

2 CORINTHIANS 12:9

Our light affliction,
which is but for a moment,
is working for us a far more exceeding
and eternal weight of glory.

2 CORINTHIANS 4:17

God's Perfect Will

When we're healthy, we easily become busy and preoccupied with the present—and end up forgetting God. But when accident or illness set us aside, we have time to reflect on what's really important. Most of all, we have time to examine our relationship to Christ, and recommit ourselves and our futures into His loving hands. Throughout the ages suffering Christians have found that the Bible's promise is true: "The Lord is near to all who call on him, to all who call on him in truth" (Psalm 145:18 NIV). The Bible also says, "The eternal God is your refuge, and underneath are the everlasting arms" (Deuteronomy 33:27 NIV).

When suffering comes, learn to trust each day into God's hands and take it as a gift from Him. In addition, even if you can't concentrate very well, let your lips be filled with prayer and praise. Yes, pray for healing; God is sovereign, and He is able to intervene. But most of all pray for His will to be done in your life—for His will is perfect.

By this we know love,
because He laid down His life for us.

1 JOHN 3:16

Love suffers long and is kind;
love does not envy; love does not parade itself,
is not puffed up; does not behave rudely,
does not seek its own, is not provoked,
thinks no evil; does not rejoice in iniquity,
but rejoices in the truth; bears all things,
believes all things, hopes all things,
endures all things.

1 CORINTHIANS 13:4–7

Beloved, let us love one another,
for love is of God; and everyone who loves
is born of God and knows God.
He who does not love does not know God,
for God is love.

1 JOHN 4:7–8

The Hallmark of Love

What the original Greek language of the New Testament called "agape" love is selfless love—love that extends even to those who aren't lovable or even worthy of love. The Bible says this is the kind of love God has for us—and is the kind of love we should have for others.

This kind of love—"agape" love—is more than a warm feeling or an impulsive act of kindness. The love God wants us to have isn't just an emotion, but a conscious act of the will—a deliberate decision on our part to put others ahead of ourselves. The Bible says, "Each of you should look not only to your own interests, but also to the interests of others" (Philippians 2:4 NIV). This is the kind of love God has for us—a love so deep that it caused Christ to leave Heaven's glory and die on the cross for us. The opposite of agape love is selfishness, but when Christ's love fills our hearts it puts selfishness on the run.

What is God's priority for you? God's priority is that His love would become the hallmark of your life—and the reason is because it was the hallmark of Christ's life.

If the Son makes you free,
you shall be free indeed.

JOHN 8:36

Forgive us our debts,
as we forgive our debtors.

MATTHEW 6:12

If you do not forgive men their trespasses,
neither will your Father forgive your trespasses.

MATTHEW 6:15

Judge not, and you shall not be judged.
Condemn not, and you shall not be condemned.
Forgive, and you will be forgiven.

LUKE 6:37

Freely Forgive

Almost every week someone writes me saying something like this: "I can't forgive. You don't know how deeply I've been hurt." Perhaps this echoes your own thoughts. But nothing releases us from the past or opens the door to reconciliation as completely as forgiveness. Even if the other person refuses to admit any fault or scorns our forgiveness, that mustn't hold us back.

The Bible is clear: "Bear with each other and forgive whatever grievances you may have against one another. Forgive as the Lord forgave you" (Colossians 3:13 NIV). Did you notice that last phrase? God forgave us freely and fully in Christ, and that's how we are to forgive others: freely and fully. It may be the hardest thing you ever do, but with God's help you can—and you must.

*Commit your way to the L*ORD,
trust also in Him,
and He shall bring it to pass.
He shall bring forth your righteousness
as the light, and your justice
as the noonday.

PSALM 37:5–6

Teach us to number our days,
that we may gain a heart of wisdom.

PSALM 90:12

*One thing I have desired of the L*ORD,
that will I seek: That I may dwell in the house
*of the L*ORD *all the days of my life,*
*to behold the beauty of the L*ORD,
and to inquire in His temple.

PSALM 27:4

The Gift of Each Day

Each day is a gift from God. It is another opportunity God has given you to serve Him. Time isn't inexhaustible, nor can we assume we'll always have more; some day our time on earth will end. The Psalmist said, "My times are in your hands" (Psalm 31:15 NIV). The first thing we should do when we awake is thank God for the gift of another day.

The second is to commit our time to God. God gave it to us for a reason: not to be wasted or mishandled, but to be used for His glory. We are accountable to Him for the way we use our time, and once a minute passes it can never be reclaimed. The Bible says, we always should be "redeeming the time, because the days are evil" (Ephesians 5:16).

Obey in all things your masters,
. . . not with eyeservice, as men-pleasers,
but in sincerity of heart, fearing God.

COLOSSIANS 3:22

Whatever your hand finds to do,
do it with your might.

ECCLESIASTES 9:10

Let the beauty of the LORD our God be upon us,
and establish the work of our hands for us;
yes, establish the work of our hands.

PSALM 90:17

From God's Hand

Instead of seeing your job as a burden, see it as a responsibility given you by God. No matter what your work is, if it is legitimate then it has dignity, for it came from God. Our work may seem burdensome and meaningless—but once we realize God gave it to us, our attitude will change. The writer of Ecclesiastes discovered this truth: "A man can do nothing better than . . . find satisfaction in his work. This too, I see, is from the hand of God" (Ecclesiastes 2:24 NIV).

We often speak of someone being "called" by God to the ministry or mission field, but if you know Christ and are in His will, you also have been called—to your vocation. (In fact, the word "vocation" comes from a Latin word meaning "to be called.") Does this mean our work will never be dull or hard or tiring? No, of course not. But when we see our work as something God gave us, even the most routine tasks take on significance.

Whatever you do, do it heartily,
as to the Lord and not to men, knowing that
from the Lord you will receive the reward
of the inheritance; for you serve the Lord Christ.

Colossians 3:23–24

LORD, You have searched me and known me.
You know my sitting down and my rising up;
You understand my thought afar off.

Psalm 139:1–2

Search me, O God, and know my heart; . . .
and lead me in the way everlasting.

Psalm 139:23–24

God Knows What Is Best

D oes God really care about the decisions we make? Does God have a plan for our lives—a plan we can actually know? Or does He expect us to make all our decisions on our own?

The Bible's answer is clear: God knows all about us, and He knows what is best for us. He sees the dangers we face, and He also knows the joys we could experience. But God not only *knows* what is best for us, He also *wants* what is best for us. The reason is simple: He loves us.

One of the most important truths I can say about God's will is this: God's will comes from God's love. If God didn't love us, He wouldn't care which way we went when we face a decision. But He does love us—and that makes all the difference. Because He loves us, we can confidently seek His will, knowing it is always best for us—*always*.

Strengthened by
God's Love

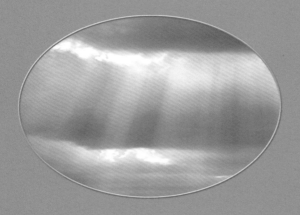

Neither death nor life, nor angels nor principalities, . . .
shall be able to separate us from the love of God.

ROMANS 8:38–39

*But grow in the grace and
knowledge of our Lord and Savior Jesus Christ.*

2 PETER 3:18

*We all, with unveiled face, beholding as
in a mirror the glory of the Lord,
are being transformed
into the same image from glory to glory,
just as by the Spirit of the Lord.*

2 CORINTHIANS 3:18

*Become blameless and pure,
children of God without fault
in a crooked and depraved generation.*

PHILIPPIANS 2:15 NIV

Growing Stronger

Many years ago (so the story goes) engineers made plans to construct a suspension bridge over a deep river gorge. The biggest problem was how to get the heavy steel cables from one side of the gorge to the other. Helicopters hadn't been invented, and the turbulent, rock-strewn river below made it too dangerous to transfer the cables by boat.

The solution? One day the engineers flew a kite over the gorge. As it hovered over the opposite shore they deliberately grounded it—which meant the two sides of the river were now linked by a thin kite string. They then tied a slightly heavier string to one end of the kite string and carefully hauled it across to the other side. Once it was in place they tied a still stronger cord to the end of that string and pulled it across. They repeated this process several more times, graduating on to stronger ropes—until eventually they were able to pull the heavy steel cables across the gorge and construct the bridge.

Spiritual growth is somewhat like the construction of that bridge. At first our faith may be small and fragile, in danger of being swept away. . . . But that isn't God's will! Just as the link between the two sides of that river gradually grew stronger and stronger, so God's will is for our faith to grow stronger and stronger. Is this happening in your life?

Create in me a clean heart,
O God, and renew a steadfast spirit within me.

PSALM 51:10

You have forgiven the iniquity of Your people;
You have covered all their sin.

PSALM 85:2

As far as the east is from the west,
so far has He removed our transgressions from us.

PSALM 103:12

In Him we have redemption
through His blood, the forgiveness of sins,
according to the riches of His grace.

EPHESIANS 1:7

Promise of Forgiveness

Sin breaks our fellowship with God—but it doesn't end our relationship. We are still His children, even when we disobey. We feel guilty and ashamed, and sometimes we simply want to hide. But God still loves us, and He wants to forgive us and welcome us back! When you fail, repent and claim God's promise of forgiveness and restoration.

The Bible promises, "If we confess our sins, he is faithful and just and will forgive us our sins and purify us from all unrighteousness" (1 John 1:9 NIV). This is God's promise to you. Believe it!

The only sin God cannot forgive is the sin of refusing His forgiveness. When you sin, don't excuse it, or ignore it, or blame it on someone else. Admit it . . . repent of it . . . and then rejoice that God has fully forgiven you.

A sound heart is life to the body,
but envy is rottenness to the bones.

PROVERBS 14:30

Keep your heart with all diligence,
for out of it spring the issues of life.

PROVERBS 4:23

The righteousness of the blameless
will direct his way aright.

PROVERBS 11:5

"He who hears My word and
believes in Him who sent Me has everlasting life,
and shall not come into judgment, but has
passed from death into life."

JOHN 5:24

Free from Sin

When King David refused to confess his adultery with Bathsheba and suppressed his feelings of guilt, he paid a price both spiritually and physically: "When I kept silent, my bones wasted away; . . . my strength was sapped" (Psalm 32:3–4 NIV). Only when he faced his sin and sought God's forgiveness did his health return. The Bible says, "A cheerful heart is good medicine, but a crushed spirit dries up the bones" (Proverbs 17:22 NIV).

Sin, like a deadly cancer, has invaded every area of our lives: our bodies, our minds, our emotions, our wills—everything. Don't take sin lightly! But Jesus Christ came to conquer sin. He came not only to forgive us; He also came to free us from sin's power and transform us by His Spirit. The Bible says, "Once you were alienated from God. . . . But now he has reconciled you . . . to present you holy in his sight, without blemish and free from accusation" (Colossians 1:21–22 NIV).

Holy . . . without blemish . . . free from accusation—this is God's purpose for you every day.

The LORD is on my side; I will not fear.

PSALM 118:6

*The LORD God is a sun and shield; the LORD will
give grace and glory; no good thing
will He withhold from those who walk uprightly.*

PSALM 84:11

*[Cast] all your care on Him,
for He cares for you.*

1 PETER 5:7

*He who dwells in the secret place
of the Most High shall abide
under the shadow of the Almighty.*

PSALM 91:1

God Is In Control

What is the opposite of fear? For the Christian there can be only one answer: The opposite of fear is trust—trust in God and His unchanging love. Once we realize God is in control and He holds us in His loving hands, we can meet life's dangers and uncertainties with confidence. After all, if we can trust God for our eternal salvation, can't we also trust Him for our lives right now?

Let's be honest, however: It's hard to trust God when danger threatens or everything seems to be collapsing around us. Fear comes much easier to us than faith. But never forget: Fear can banish faith, but faith can banish fear. Faith isn't pretending our problems don't exist, nor is it simply blind optimism. Faith points us beyond our problems to the hope we have in Christ. True faith involves trust—trust in what Christ has done for us, and trust in God's goodness and mercy.

*"In the world you will have tribulation;
but be of good cheer, I have overcome the world."*

JOHN 16:33

*There has not failed one word
of all His good promise.*

1 KINGS 8:56

*You know in all your hearts
and in all your souls that not one thing
has failed of all the good things which
the LORD your God spoke concerning you.
All have come to pass for you;
not one word of them has failed.*

JOSHUA 23:14

The Promises of God

In the Bible God has given us "very great and precious promises" (2 Peter 1:4 NIV)—and every one of them reminds us that we can trust our lives into His hands. You can trust God's promises, for He cannot lie! God's promises in the Old Testament are just as applicable and relevant to us today as those in the New Testament, and both Testaments contain God's principles for life. Fear vanishes when it is exposed to the promises of God's Word.

What are those promises? One is that God is with you, no matter how difficult or confusing life becomes. He says, "Never will I leave you; never will I forsake you" (Hebrews 13:5 NIV). Jesus declared, "Surely I am with you always, to the very end of the age" (Matthew 28:20 NIV). You are never alone if you know Christ—never. I have never forgotten the familiar words from Psalm 23 my mother taught me as a child: "Yea, though I walk through the valley of the shadow of death, I will fear no evil: for Thou art with me; Thy rod and Thy staff they comfort me" (Psalm 23:4 KJV). Saturate your mind and heart with the promises of God's Word.

*"Shall God not avenge His own
elect who cry out
day and night to Him,
though He bears long with them?"*

Luke 18:7

*In my distress I called upon the LORD,
and cried out to my God;
He heard my voice from His temple,
and my cry entered His ears.*

2 Samuel 22:7

*Rest in the LORD,
and wait patiently for Him.*

Psalm 37:7

Our Faithful God

One of the most frequent questions people ask me concerns unanswered prayer. "God must be deaf," someone bluntly wrote me. "My prayers never get above the ceiling," another wrote. But God knows what is best for us, and we need to learn to trust Him for the outcome. Sometimes God answers "Yes" when we ask Him for something. But sometimes His answer is "Not yet," or even "No." And sometimes His answer is simply "Trust me, even if you don't understand."

Ruth's father, Dr. Bell, always kept a list of people for whom he was praying. After his death Ruth found one of his prayer lists ("Mostly illegible," she commented; "you know how doctors write!"). On it was a specific concern about one of our children. Not until five years after his death was that prayer answered—a vivid reminder of God's faithfulness in answering prayer according to His timetable, not ours.

Many are the afflictions of the righteous,
but the LORD delivers him out of them all.

PSALM 34:19

I will cry out to God Most High,
to God who performs all things for me.

PSALM 57:2

If any of you lacks wisdom, let him ask
of God, who gives to all liberally
and without reproach,
and it will be given to him.

JAMES 1:5

Praying always with all prayer and
supplication in the Spirit,
being watchful to this end with
all perseverance.

EPHESIANS 6:18

Fear Not

The Bible's answer to worry couldn't be clearer: "Do not be anxious about anything, but in everything, by prayer and petition, with thanksgiving, present your requests to God." Then comes God's promise: "And the peace of God, which transcends all understanding, will guard your hearts and your minds in Christ Jesus" (Philippians 4:6–7 NIV).

How should you pray? Pray first of all for strength in the face of whatever you fear, for God helps us hold on in the midst of life's storms. Pray also for wisdom to deal with whatever is worrying you; some practical steps may change the situation.

Pray as well that God will act to change your circumstances, according to His will. He doesn't always do what we want Him to—but He knows what's best for us, and He can be trusted. God is sovereign, and no situation is beyond His control. Over her desk my wife has these words: "Fear not the future; God is already there."

*By humility and the fear of the L<small>ORD</small>
are riches and honor and life.*

P ROVERBS 22:4

*All of you be submissive to one another,
and be clothed with humility,
for "God resists the proud,
but gives grace to the humble."*

1 P ETER 5:5

*Being found in appearance as a man,
He humbled Himself and
became obedient to the point of death,
even the death of the cross.*

P HILIPPIANS 2:8

Christ–Our Example

One of the most memorable experiences of my life was the opportunity to visit a remote mountainous corner of India called Nagaland. Nagaland has one of the largest concentrations of Christians in India, and the occasion was the 100th anniversary of the coming of missionaries to that area. Tens of thousands came to the celebration—some walking for days over rough jungle trails. 100,000 people, we were told, would be gathering each morning for a Bible study, in addition to the evening evangelistic meetings.

When we arrived at Government House where we were to stay a man unloaded our baggage from the car, then took our shoes to wipe the mud off them. I protested, saying we could do that, but he insisted. Only later did I discover that he would be leading the Bible study for those 100,000 people the next morning! Here was a man who truly exemplified the attitude of Christ by his humility and his willingness to serve others. I have never forgotten his example.

Be strong and of good courage;
do not be afraid,
nor be dismayed, for the LORD your God
is with you wherever you go.

JOSHUA 1:9

In the fear of the LORD there is strong confidence,
and His children will have a place of refuge.

PROVERBS 14:26

He said to me,
"My grace is sufficient for you, for My strength
is made perfect in weakness."

2 CORINTHIANS 12:9

Character Counts

Parts of the Great Wall date back before Christ, and it still stretches across hundreds of miles of rugged mountainous terrain. It remains one of the most remarkable construction projects in history, and is, I'm told, one of the few man-made objects visible from space. It was built for one purpose: to keep out barbarians bent on destroying Chinese civilization.

At first the Great Wall was a success; its height and well-guarded gates repelled every invasion. But eventually the enemy succeeded. How? The solution was simple: They found a gatekeeper of weak character and bribed him into leaving his gate unlocked.

Our lives are often like the Great Wall: strong and fortified at some points—but weak and vulnerable at others. And where will Satan attack? Not where he knows we are strong and he stands no chance of victory. A chain is only as strong as its weakest link, and so is our character. Know your weaknesses, and then with God's help turn them into strengths.

How precious is Your lovingkindness,
O God! Therefore the children of men put their
trust under the shadow of Your wings.

PSALM 36:7

I have not hidden Your righteousness
within my heart; I have declared Your faithfulness
and Your salvation.

PSALM 40:10

Though He slay me,
yet will I trust Him.

JOB 13:15

All-Powerful and Loving

None of us will ever forget September 11, 2001. Within minutes our world changed forever as two hijacked airliners plowed into the twin towers of America's tallest building, the World Trade Center in New York City, and a third slammed into the Pentagon in Washington.

I was invited by the President to speak three days later at a special service of prayer and remembrance in Washington's National Cathedral. What could I say to bring comfort and hope to a nation in crisis?

"I have been asked hundreds of times in my life why God allows tragedy and suffering," I told the congregation that day. "I really do not know the answer totally, even to my own satisfaction. I have to accept, by faith, that God is sovereign, and He is a God of love and mercy and compassion in the midst of suffering."

Does that sound like a contradiction? Perhaps it does, at least to our limited minds. Yet both are true: Evil is real—but so is God's power and love. And because He is all-powerful and loving we can cling to Him in trust and faith, even when we don't understand.

We are hard-pressed on every side,
but not crushed;
we are perplexed, but not in despair.

2 CORINTHIANS 4:8

You, O LORD, are a God full
of compassion, and gracious, longsuffering and
abundant in mercy and truth.

PSALM 86:15

The eternal God is your refuge,
and underneath are the everlasting arms.

DEUTERONOMY 33:27

God Understands Suffering

Evil and suffering are real, whether we see them on our television screens or confront them in the privacy of our own lives. They aren't an illusion, nor are they simply an absence of good. None of us is immune from their grasp; suffering and tragedy touch us all, no matter who we are.

But God is also real! He is just as real as our pain and heartache—and even more so, for some day they will vanish, but He will still remain. In the midst of life's tragedies He wants to assure us of His presence and love—even if we don't understand why He allowed them to happen. He knows what we are going through, for He experienced evil's fiercest assault when His beloved Son suffered the pangs of death and Hell. God understands our suffering, for Christ endured far greater suffering than we ever will. The cross tells us that God understands our pain and confusion—but more than that, it tells us He loves us, and He will never abandon us.

Shaped by God's Love

God is love.

1 John 4:8

*I know the thoughts that I think toward you,
says the* LORD, *thoughts of peace and not of evil,
to give you a future and a hope.*

JEREMIAH 29:11

*He knows the way that I take;
when He has tested me,
I shall come forth as gold.*

JOB 23:10

Trust in the LORD *with all your heart,
and lean not on your own understanding;
in all your ways acknowledge Him,
and He shall direct your paths.*

PROVERBS 3:5–6

God's Perfect Plan

One of the happiest days of my life was when Ruth said she would be my wife. I could hardly contain my joy! But only a few years before I had faced one of the saddest days of my life, when another fine young woman with whom I thought I would be spending the rest of my life suddenly broke off our relationship. I was brokenhearted, convinced she must be making a mistake— but God knew better. Ruth was God's choice for me (just as I was God's choice for her), and I will always be grateful for His goodness in saving us for each other.

God has a personal, individual plan for each of us. It embraces the big things in life: who we will marry, what our career will be, where we will live, even when we will die. It also includes the details of our daily lives: decisions about our families, finances, leisure time, friendships, and countless other choices we make. No matter what decisions you are facing, seek His will—for His way is always best.

The fruit of the Spirit is love, joy, peace,
patience, kindness, goodness,
faithfulness, gentleness, self-control. . . .
If we live in the Spirit,
let us also walk in the Spirit.

GALATIANS 5:22–25

Let us not love in word or in tongue,
but in deed and in truth.
And by this we know that we are of the truth,
and shall assure our hearts before Him.

1 JOHN 3:18–19

This is love, that we walk
according to His commandments.

2 JOHN 6

Shaped by God's Love

God doesn't want to erase our personalities—although He does want to take the sharp edges off them! We are all different, because God made us that way. Saul of Tarsus had what we today might call a "Type A" personality—hard-driving, determined, energetic, absolutely focused on his goal of destroying the Christian faith. But God intervened and replaced Saul's hatred of Christ with love. His basic personality didn't change, but God redirected his energies and used him instead (as the Apostle Paul) to advance the Gospel.

Paul's young companion Timothy, on the other hand, had a different personality—shy, sensitive, perhaps even a bit introverted. But God helped Timothy overcome his shyness so he could reach out to others, and God also used his sensitive nature to make him an effective and caring pastor. Thank God for making you the unique person you are, and ask Him to shape you and use you according to His will.

Teach me Your way, O Lord;
I will walk in Your truth;
unite my heart to fear Your name.

Psalm 86:11

I have not departed from Your judgments,
for You Yourself have taught me.

Psalm 119:102

You have commanded us
to keep Your precepts diligently.
Oh, that my ways
were directed to keep Your statutes!

Psalm 119:4–5

Guidance for Life

When a soldier submits to the authority of his commanding officer, he obeys what that officer tells him to do. If a patient submits to a doctor's treatment, he or she does what the doctor says to do. If a football player submits to the direction of his coach, he does what the coach instructs him to do. And when we submit ourselves to the King of kings and the Lord of lords, we obey what He tells us to do, because we know His way is right.

God shows us His will first of all through His Word, the Bible. How many problems would we avoid if we knew God's Word and obeyed it? The Bible doesn't give us a rule for every conceivable situation—but it does cover far more than most of us realize. It also gives us principles by which we are to guide our lives. God's Word isn't to be debated or dissected; it is to be *done*.

May our Lord Jesus Christ Himself,
and our God and Father, who has loved us
and given us everlasting consolation
and good hope by grace,
comfort your hearts and establish you
in every good word and work.

2 THESSALONIANS 2:16–17

By this you know the Spirit of God:
Every spirit that confesses that Jesus Christ
has come in the flesh is of God.

1 JOHN 4:2

He Himself is our peace. . . .
for through Him we both have access
by one Spirit to the Father.

EPHESIANS 2:14,18

Three In One

The Bible clearly teaches that God comes to us in three distinct ways: as Father, Son and Holy Spirit. At the end of one of his letters Paul wrote, "May the grace of the Lord Jesus Christ, and the love of God, and the fellowship of the Holy Spirit be with you all" (2 Corinthians 13:14 NIV). All three—Father, Son and Holy Spirit—are distinct, and yet they are also united as one. We do not worship three Gods (as Christians have sometimes been accused of doing); we worship one God, who reveals Himself to us in three persons.

How can we visualize this? When St. Patrick first brought Christianity to Ireland, it is said that he used a clover leaf to explain the Trinity to new converts: three separate leaves, and yet combined in only one plant. Others have used the sun to illustrate the Trinity: The sun is an object in space, but it also produces both light and heat—and yet it is still one. Water can be a solid, or a liquid, or a gas—but it is all water. Sometimes when I go into a church I notice what are called "trefoil" windows—windows in the form of three interlocking circles. Each circle is separate, and yet together they form a single design, symbolizing the Trinity. A mystery? Yes—but also a source of great comfort.

Surely goodness and mercy shall follow me
all the days of my life;
and I will dwell in the house
of the LORD forever.

PSALM 23:6

I know that my Redeemer lives,
and He shall stand at last on the earth;
and after my skin is destroyed, this I know,
that in my flesh I shall see God.

JOB 19:25–26

"I am the resurrection and the life.
He who believes in Me, though he may die,
he shall live."

JOHN 11:25

A Glorious Promise!

In Heaven we will be like Christ. Some day God's plan to make us more like Christ will be complete, for "we will all be changed—in a flash, in the twinkling of an eye, at the last trumpet" (1 Corinthians 15:51–52 NIV).

What does this mean? First, it means we will have new bodies—bodies that will be like Christ's resurrection body. Do I know what we'll look like in Heaven? No—but our new bodies will be perfect, beyond the reach of all illness and decay.

It also means our whole nature will be transformed. Some day we will be like Christ! Now we love imperfectly—but not then. Now our joy and peace are tempered by sorrow and turmoil—but not then. The Bible says, "Dear friends, now we are children of God, and what we will be has not yet been made known. But we know that when he appears, we shall be like him, for we shall see him as he is" (1 John 3:2 NIV). What a glorious promise!

*I must work the works of Him
who sent Me while it is day.*

JOHN 9:4

We know . . . we shall be like Him.

1 JOHN 3:2

Our citizenship is in heaven.

PHILIPPIANS 3:20

*We, according to His promise,
look for new heavens and a new earth
in which righteousness dwells.*

2 PETER 3:13

Heaven Is Real

Life is hard—but God is good and Heaven is real." This is what a doctor friend of mine sometimes tells his Christian patients, because he knows how easily we get caught up in our present problems and forget God's promise of Heaven. Paul wrote, "If only for this life we have hope in Christ, we are to be pitied more than all men" (1 Corinthians 15:19 NIV). But our hope isn't only for this life! In the midst of life's storms, our hope in God's promise of Heaven is "an anchor for the soul, firm and secure" (Hebrews 6:19 NIV).

When we know Christ, we know life isn't meaningless, because God has a reason for keeping us here. Every day is a gift from Him, and is another opportunity to love Him and serve Him. Heaven doesn't make this life *less* important; it makes it *more* important.

"In my Father's house are many mansions;
if it were not so, I would have told you.
I go to prepare a place for you.
And if I go and prepare a place for you,
I will come again and receive you to Myself;
that where I am, there you may be also."

JOHN 14:2–3

The Lord will deliver me from
every evil work and preserve me for
His heavenly kingdom.

2 TIMOTHY 4:18

I know whom I have believed and
am persuaded that He is able to keep what I have
committed to Him until that Day.

2 TIMOTHY 1:12

Our Sure Hope

Why did Jesus Christ leave Heaven's glory and enter this sin-infested world? For one reason: to make our eternal salvation possible. When God created Adam and Eve, His plan was that they would live in perfect harmony with Him forever. But Satan was determined to change that, and with his lies he lured them away from God. When that happened, death came upon the human race, and we are all its victims. Never forget: Death was Satan's greatest victory.

But by His death and resurrection Jesus Christ reversed this. Satan's greatest victory has now been turned into defeat! Death has now been put to death! No wonder the Bible says, "Where, O death, is your victory? Where, O death, is your sting? . . . Thanks be to God! He gives us the victory through our Lord Jesus Christ" (1 Corinthians 15:55, 57 NIV).

Christ's motive in coming to earth was love, and His goal was to destroy death and take us to be with the Father forever. This is our sure hope.

We know that if our earthly house, this tent,
is destroyed, we have a building from God,
a house not made with hands,
eternal in the heavens.

2 CORINTHIANS 5:1

Rejoice because your names are written in heaven.

LUKE 10:20

We are . . .
pleased rather to be absent from the body
and to be present with the Lord.

2 CORINTHIANS 5:8

With God Forever!

Heaven is many things—but the most important is this: Heaven is God's dwelling place. It is the place where God lives! It's true that God is everywhere—but Heaven is more than a place; it is a whole different dimension of existence, and God is in its midst, with Christ at His right hand. The Bible says, "we will be with the Lord forever" (1 Thessalonians 4:17 NIV).

Think of it: We will be with God forever! And because we will be with Him, we will be absolutely safe from all evil. Sorrow and suffering will never again touch us—never. One of the most moving passages in all the Bible is found in its next to last chapter: "And I heard a loud voice from the throne saying, 'Now the dwelling of God is with men, and he will live with them. They will be his people, and God himself will be with them and be their God. He will wipe away every tear from their eyes. There will be no more death or mourning or crying or pain, for the old order of things has passed away'" (Revelation 21:3–4 NIV). Praise God for the hope we have in Christ!